Wheat Farm Press
Print Exchange 1:1
January 2011

Participants
Dan Alvarado
Bill Brookover
Sabrina Cacciatorie
Kathryn Cellerini
Michael Connors
Aimee Denault
Esther Kwon
Justin Mages
Alisha McCurdy
Aaron Miller
Jose Antonio Ojeda
Krystal Read
Jonathan Stewart
Nicole Suchy
Ariana Warner
Si Wu

Guest Curator
Matthew Brown

Guest Writer
Meredith Stern

Editor/ Director
Julianne Gadoury

©Wheat Farm Press
January 2011
all artwork is copyright by the
individual artists
ISBN-13: 978-1460921319

ISBN-10: 1460921313

Letter from the Director:

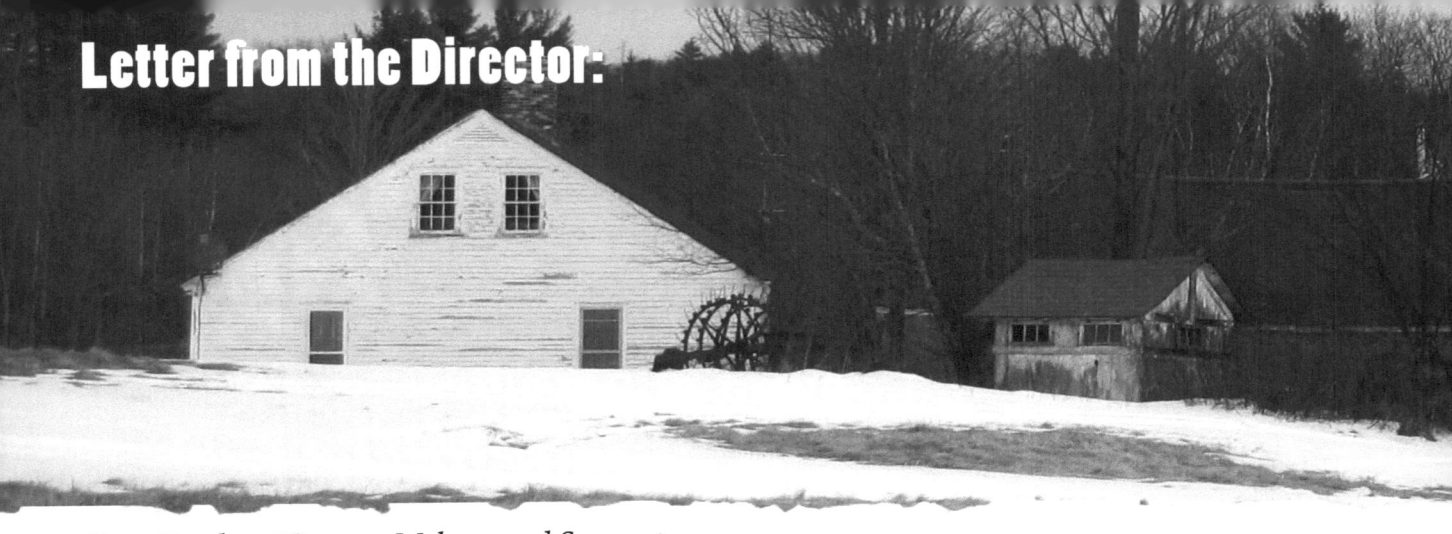

Dear Readers, Viewers, Makers, and Supporters:

Here is the catalog of the inaugural Wheat Farm Press Print Exchange 1:1. Participants and subscribers have helped to make history, and collectively build a great start for our organization. For this first print exchange we had a total of sixteen participants who are engaged with printmaking in many different forms, and are from all over the United States. We have participants who are students, established professors and artists, and those who print whenever they get a chance! Prints were sent to the Wheat Farm from California, New York, Wisconsin, Arizona, New Jersey, Texas, and Indiana. We couldn't be happier with the beautiful and eclectic range of prints and participants that we received for this first exchange.

The goal of Wheat Farm Press is to eventually gain non-profit status. Until then we are operating like a non-profit, and putting any profits toward quality essayists for the publication, curators, and gaining exhibition space. We would eventually like to purchase a press so that we can establish an artist in residence program. We would like to invite artists to the Wheat Farm in New Hampshire for uninterrupted time to devote to printmaking. In exchange, we are hoping to build on relationships with local youth organizations where artists would work on projects with youth for one afternoon a week.

We have decided to publish all the prints received for the exchange for this publication. Congratulations to everyone! The magazine will start with a conversation between myself and Providence, RI based artist and musician, Meredith Stern. The guest curator, woodblock artist Matthew Brown, chose the cover image. We are hoping for the magazine to grow into a record of what is happening in printmaking now, and as a record of what is being created for the purpose of exchange. Our next quarterly magazine will feature an essay on the nature of exchange.

Please help us grow, and encourage any fellow printmakers you know to participate in this wonderful activity. Together, we are helping to deepen the roots of a strong printmaking community through an exchange of ideas, artistic output, and practice.

Cheers from the Wheat Farm!

Julianne Gadoury
Director
Wheat Farm Press

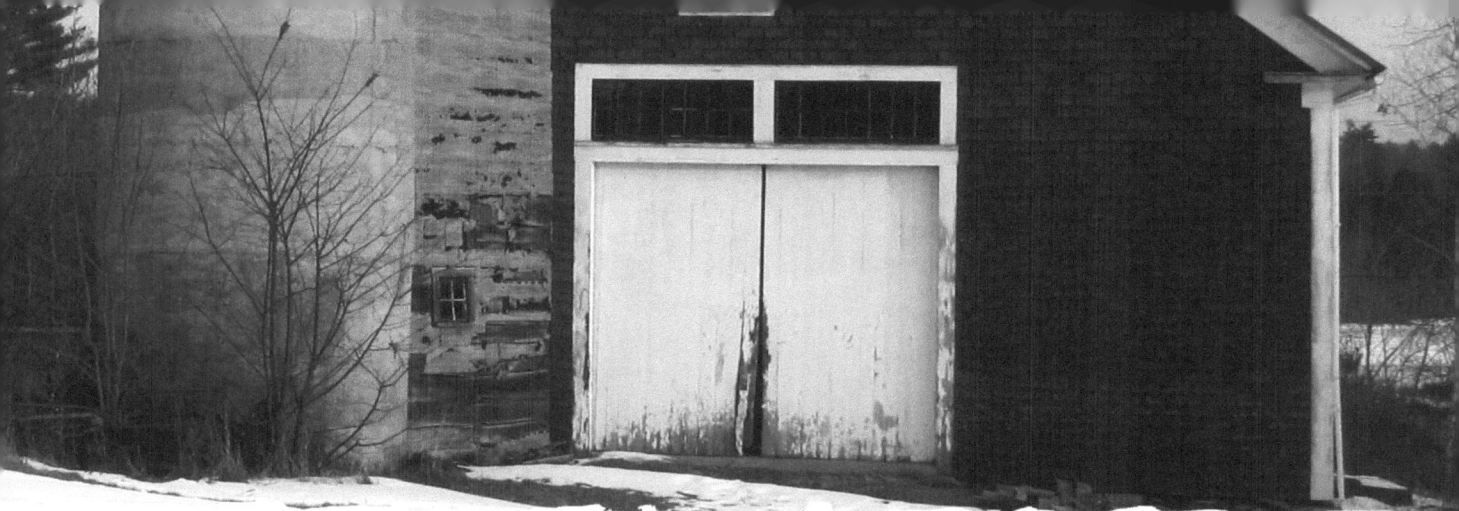

On the cover: Krystal Read, *Memories Racing 'Round (detail)*, intaglio

" I have chosen Krystal Read's Memories Racing 'Round as the most interesting print to me. I have chosen it for its pictorial theme, with an interesting variety of formal elements and technical approaches to the subject matter." -Matt Brown, guest curator

Matt Brown: I began my work with color woodblock printing in 1993, soon after the birth of our first son Nathaniel. I am primarily self-taught. My craft is the result of inspiration, frustration, help from other printmakers both dead and living, and a lot of work. I feel grateful to pursue a craft that is non-toxic, relies on the basic materials of wood and water, and has a small carbon footprint!

Matt Brown's woodblock prints can be found in New Hampshire at six League of New Hampshire Craftsmen retail shops, Long river studios, Mary McGowan Fine Art, The Old Print Barn, and many other retail galleries throughout New England. www.mattbrown.biz

Wheat Farm Press: The Beginnings

Providence, RI based artist and musician, Meredith Stern, talks with Wheat Farm Press founder and director Julianne Gadoury

One morning I received an unexpected e-mail from Julianne, who had read a conversation between printmakers that I moderated called "Subversive Multiples" which appears in the book, "Realizing the Impossible: Art Against Authority" edited by Josh MacPhee and Erik Ruin on AK Press. Julianne informed me she was starting a project that sounded interesting- a printmaking project located in an old farm. This project is currently starting as a farm with an enthusiastic printmaker looking to delve into some print related group projects that will engage a larger community of artists and young people. Julianne graciously asked me to write a forward to introduce her project, to write an essay expressing my ideas about the accessibility of printmaking. She also explained that her first project would be to put together a juried journal. I was intrigued by the offer to write a forward, but was more interested in engaging in a dialogue instead. So, what follows is a brief e-mail exchange we had. Through reading this, you will hear our thoughts on printmaking and creative process, and also an understanding about the motivation behind Wheat Farm Press. We begin with a question that I brought up upon learning that the first project of Wheat Farm would be to create a juried portfolio project.

How would you argue that a juried exhibition/portfolio would promote accessibility in the arts? For me, these two ideas: "jurying" and "accessibility" are at odds with one another. Accessibility has many meanings: first, is whether artists are able to participate, and second, how the art is distributed and made available to a public. Jurying work means that artists are competing with one another for re-sources/representation; and while that follows the norm that has been established within the elite Main-stream art world, to me, it is a norm that I prefer to rebel against. I myself prefer to exhibit in either curated shows- where a curator specifically picks out several artists whose work they would like to show together- or an open call that allows all artists to participate. I have made a conscious effort to avoid juried exhibitions. To me, juried events represent a maintenance of the status quo in the art world- which means limiting access. White men are still chosen at a higher proportion in juried competitions than women, people of color, LGBT folks. It also raises the issue as to who is encouraged to participate from day one in the art world-- predominately white, wealthy, males are represented the most in the art world, which begins when we are children and continues throughout our schooling and is quite obvious when looking at the hard data as to whose work dominates in the modern art world. White male children are still offered the most resources, support, schooling, and connections in the art world as children/teens/college students/adults. So, to me, increasing accessibility in the art world ties in with something you touched on-- drawing in more youth as a start. But also, in providing more opportunities for people who need more assistance in accessing the art world. I believe that one way of overcoming this imbalance is by promoting projects that are open to everyone, regardless of experience or a uniform standard as to what makes "good work." So, I am curious on your thoughts on these things.   --Meredith

Your feelings toward art being juried is a perspective that I hadn't thought about before, but I do agree with many of your reasons to rebel against it. What are the goals of Wheat Farm Press? It has been my dream to establish an artist's residency and community organization. Hence, Wheat Farm Press has been born, and eventually a larger organization Wheat Farm Studio Workshop will hopefully evolve out of it. Organizations in rural settings can help their communities by employing local artisans as teachers for workshops, and by encouraging community members at all age levels to participate in different forms of creation. An arts organization in a rural environment would highlight regional cultural history, as well as provide a form of arts education that would reinforce community participation and interaction. Many public school systems have cut their arts budgets so youth might not have any access to the arts growing up, or only part time access. No access as youth, means no appreciation as adults. I believe you have to practice creativity, just as you have to practice football, to do well at it. If youth are never given the opportunity to express themselves creatively, and make creative decisions, then I deeply believe they will have trouble later in life in any problem solving situation. Art allows for a direct expression of each individual soul, and not simply trying out different variables that fit into a formula. We need creativity in all areas of life, no matter what age we are. Participating in the arts also allows for youth to develop a sense of the many amazing things they are capable of. What happens when there is no right answer, when there is no grade on the test? With art, and life there often is no "right answer" so each individual learns to create to their best possible abilities, and only they will know if they have worked their hardest, and to their full potential. This quality is another trait that will be useful later in life, and help to develop hardworking honest community members. Without the arts, we develop as a community who does not know how to think for itself, and only knows how to operate through life when a prescription is written for them. The arts can serve as a meaningful hobby that can enhance quality of life, if not participating in them, but simply appreciating a play, an art exhibit, or a community concert.

Why is Wheat Farm Press establishing a print exchange and juried publication? Wheat Farm Press is in its infancy. In order to eventually grow into non-profit status, and purchase equipment like a press, and be able to invite artists for a residency, we need to start somewhere. Wheat Farm Press is basically a flat file, a Wheat Farm, and a mailbox. Our goal however is to involve highly skilled and passionate artists, designers, and writers in our projects, in order to give as many people the opportunity to participate as possible. I love print exchanges, and the idea behind them. I love the idea of creating an edition with the simple intent of sharing, and not for any commercial or personal gain. Why a juried publication? You said that you feel juried exhibitions/ publications are forcing artists into competition for exposure and resources. Although that largely is true, perhaps this publication could be thought of as a celebration of what was accomplished through the print exchange. My goal with this exchange is for everyone to put their best foot forward. Idealistic, I know, but I don't want people participating just to get something in return. Obviously, every one of us has a million different commitments that make up our lives, and can possibly take away from reaching our fullest artistic potential. Also, as artists we theoretically would never be completely satisfied with a single work, and that is why we keep creating. Unfortunately however, I have found in some exchanges some people put forward a less than honest effort at creating an image. They don't give it their all, and instead take an easy simpler route. With this exchange, I want people to challenge themselves to create the best possible image that they can, given their own personal variables such as time and resources. When putting forth your best effort, you show respect to the entire printmaking community, that you are adding your artistic voice to the community in order to benefit everyone. Much as a conversation can produce fuller more diverse results than one

person simply rattling off their own opinion. The blind juried publication would highlight the most exemplary prints that were received from the entire exchange. This would allow for sharing of ideas again, as everyone will only receive ten physical prints back, but could also relatively cheaply receive a journal of reproduced images demonstrating the best skills or advanced ideas. This publication will serve as record of creation for a given time period, which I also believe is historically important. This will always be a blind jury, and I will work hard to invite jurors, designers, and writers from diverse backgrounds. Maybe the words juror and competition, need to be rethought. I do completely agree that the best resources are still given to white males. To repeat again some of the beliefs expressed above, if the arts are not accessible to everyone- or even valued by a community, then they are seen as superfluous. Do we want a world in which the only people who have time or access to creative thought or leisure activities, are those who don't have to work to survive? I have taught in the arts from middle school aged youth through the college level, and often the spoiled youth wants everything done for them in the arts as well. They don't know the value of work, and therefore, don't know how to set and attain a high standard for themselves. The arts community cannot flourish if only one opinion is being expressed. By assuring access to the arts by every diverse member of our nation, then we help to maintain a democratic free nation. By giving everyone the fair opportunity to express themselves we enhance the quality of life for the entire country. Does this relationship of creativity and quality of life make sense?
– Julianne

I agree with you that young people need access to the art world, and I think it's one of the largest tragedies to our youth that so many schools are cutting arts funding out of their budgets. I think that art is a great way for people of all ages to engage in dialog with other people- but also, on a basic level, as one of the most direct ways they can express themselves. The beauty of creativity is that there are so many ways to communicate: through words in a poem, or in the visual picture of a painting, or through the physical dimensions of a sculpture. I do think that it is important for people of any age who are just beginning to speak through their art, to be able to experiment without fear of being judged or compete with other artists. What ideas do you have as to specific programs you would like to create for youth? In terms of the jurying of work, it takes time (often a lifetime!) for a person to develop their own style, voice, and a sense of confidence in their work. I think it can be detrimental to an artist's development if they put their art work up to be judged and are not ready to be (potentially) rejected. I think that the most important role of art is the making of it. Although it is very flattering to have an audience appreciate your work, so few artists gain recognition for their work that the largest reward must come in the actual act of creating. A phrase you use that I really like is "Participating in the arts also allows for youth to develop a sense of the many amazing things they are capable of." I think this is the best scenario that can be created for youth; or anyone who expresses their ideas through an art form. I would argue that all creative expression is important and crucial to the health and well being of our society as a whole, and of the individuals within it. It can be a deeply shattering process for a developing artist to be told that their art is underdeveloped, or not good. Few people (if any?) have an innate talent for being able to express their idea exactly as it appears in their mind. Each piece we create helps us further develop our voice, so I believe there are no failures in art. It surprised me then, when you state that, "I have found in some exchanges some people put forward a less than honest effort at creating an image. They don't give it their all." I would argue that all artistic expression is worthy, and that it's unfair to use universal standards when judging creative output. When we look at the multitude of cultures around the world, aesthetics vary greatly around the world. What constitutes art that is considered good in one region may be considered low art in another, and vice versa. Even within the "Modern Art" world, there is no consensus of "what is art". For some curators, art that presents a strong concept maybe more important than how the idea is expressed, and for others, the technical aspects of using a medium can be more important than the need to communicate a specific concept. But who are we to judge that one may be called art and the other not? By your own standards, how would you determine what makes a piece of art "exemplary"?

I do believe that portfolio projects are a very powerful way for people to share their art with other people, and a print exchange can be a great way for artists to connect with each other, and to build a community. But, there are ways of creating a print exchange -mainly, an open call- that does not limit the accessibility, and can create a stronger and more vibrant community. You say, very eloquently, "The arts community cannot flourish if only one opinion is being expressed." Jurying work presents this very issue. It gives one person (or a couple, in the case of co-jurying) the power to determine what is "good" art, and to set the tone for what is considered an appropriate form of expression. It would seem to me that it would be very exciting if the first event you had was an open call for art, rather than a juried event. It would also provide a way for people to come to the Wheat Farm, meet you, see the space, and get excited about the possibilities for what

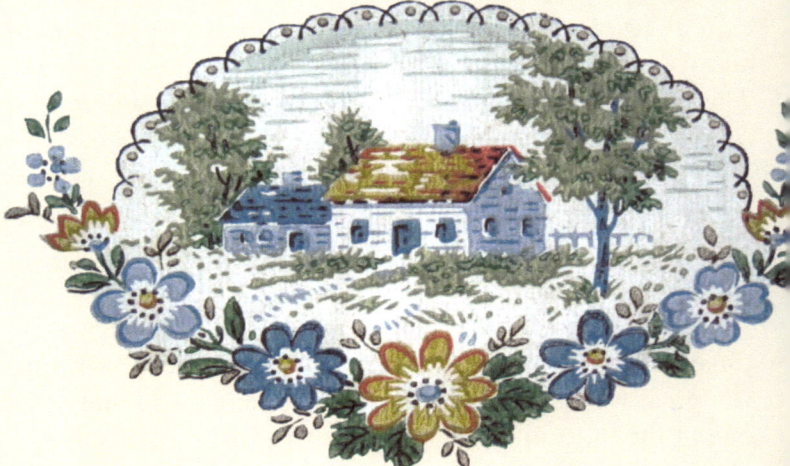

will be possible with more resources. You might meet other local artists who know of equipment that needs a home, or find people who want to donate time, money, or other resources that can help you build a space with direct local community support. I have found that the group projects I have been a part of to be far more rewarding than projects I take on alone. Have you connected with the larger community in which you live, and are you embarking on this project with assistance from other people? Do you have co-conspirators in this project?
-Meredith

This print exchange was developed as a first project that I could work on with minimal resources (money and physical help). I want to get the ball rolling in establishing an organization, even if it starts at a snail's speed. I have received support and advice for the project from many close friends who collectively have been involved with all aspects of organizing art events and programming.. My desire was never to have this be a solo project, and I deeply believe that each individual has a different set of skills that when combined with others' unique talents can build a strong organization. I don't know how long it will take for Wheat Farm Press to grow into something more than a print exchange. We'd like to buy a press, and invite artists up to produce work and interact with the community. I love models of artist in residences like Women's Studio Workshop where artists work with a local school for 6 weeks teaching students a specific medium. I think it is really enriching when an artist can engage with the community for a longer period of time, and develop a relationship. We would also like to provide classes for the community that are taught by the community. I just moved back to central New Hampshire, and have been continuously meeting people who are interested in, and support the arts. Until Wheat Farm Press grows into something more, I will continually be trying to involve different people in every aspect of the print exchange and publication. I am aiming for jurors, writers, designers from different backgrounds each quarter in order to not only provide opportunities for those involved, but create a different recipe each time of what converges into the publication.

The quarterly print exchange came about after I had been reading about print clubs that met during the 1920's in China. The young Chinese artists were searching for a new artistic medium that was accessible to the masses, and that also wasn't elitist, in that you didn't have to go to art school to study and appreciate the art form. These print clubs would require members to develop 3 new prints to be discussed at bi-weekly meetings. I was inspired reading about these clubs, and the amount of work that they were producing, especially with other obligations of life knocking at their door in the lead up to the Sino-Japanese war. Similar situations can be seen in Mexico, where the rise of printmaking in the 1920s and 1930s produced unbelievable amounts of new impassioned work. I want to not only celebrate the history of exchange and accessibility of printmaking, but help to further cement this strong community that we have. The annual events that printmaking as a medium draws people from all over the world to attend are amazing: the Mid America Print Council Conference, Southern Graphics Council Conference, Editions and Artists Book Fair, The Print Fair, and more. As a teacher, I am always looking for examples of contemporary prints that might not be seen in galleries or museums. Like you said, "So few artists gain recognition for their work, that the largest reward must come in the actual act of creating." This publication is another opportunity to see prints being created by artists who don't already have lots of exposure. I don't want you to think I'm missing your point on jurying, because I do agree with your point that it can be limiting, and imposing a small group of people's idea of what is "good" upon the entire pool of participants. Anytime you have one person or multiple people choose work to be included in something, it will exclude work solely on individual preference. Ideally, Wheat Farm Press would love to put together a publication every quarter of all the prints that were submitted to the exchange. This however would get very expensive, and would in turn make the publication inaccessible, because the high cost would exclude some people from purchasing and owning the publication. Perhaps a publication could made with all submissions that was available at a higher price, and if interested institutions wanted to purchase it for community access, like at a library that would be beneficial. After this publication, I will have to rethink the title of juror. I see the publication as a celebration of the exchange, highlighting a select number of pieces as an archive of artistic production at a period of time in history, and as an archive of work created for the sole intent of exchange. Your opinions on jurying I believe are important for the entire arts community, and by having this discussion, forces myself and hopefully others to think more about what it means to participate in something that has a selection process. If the arts are to thrive within any culture, then rules for participation that have been established need to be questioned. By placing rules for participation upon ourselves, we are only limiting the amount of accessibility to the arts for everyone.
-Julianne Gadoury

Meredith Stern currently lives in Providence RI where she lays ink onto linoleum, spins clay on a pottery wheel, and bangs the drums all in the comfort of her own home. She's a part of the Justseeds Artist Cooperative (online at http://www.justseeds.org) and works as the Program Director at AS220. Meredith lives with her sweetheart Peter Glantz, and two cats Jello and Gandalf.

Julianne Gadoury is the founder and director of Wheat Farm Press. She is committed to the belief that the arts can enhance quality of life, and is working to create arts opportunities for others. She has taught college level basic printmaking and foundations of drawing as well as worked with many non-profit arts organizations. Her own artwork helps her explore and understand social events. www.juliannegadoury.com

Opposite:
Meredith Stern, *Sustainable Growth*. Linoleum and Woodblock, 18"x 24" edition of 50

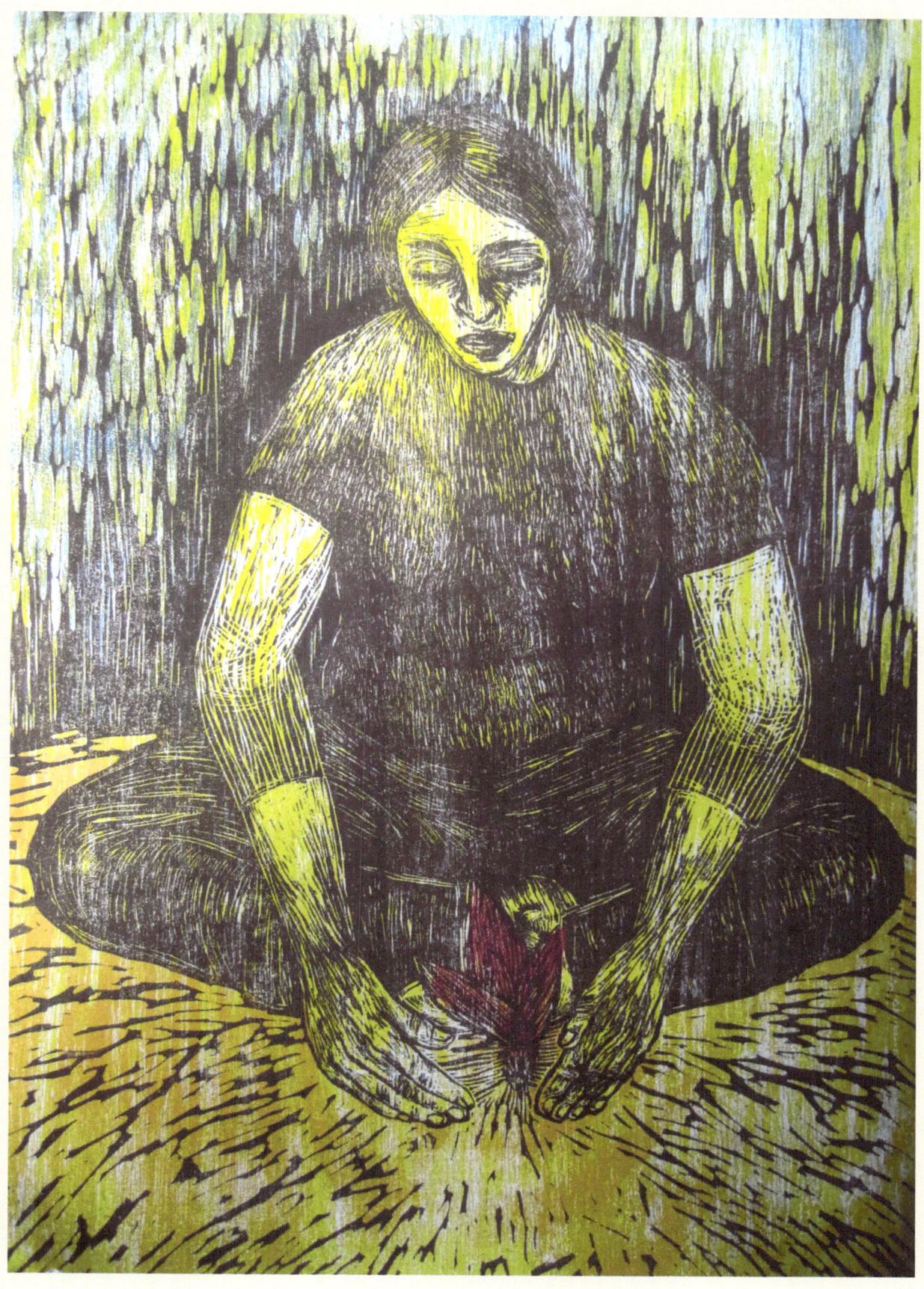

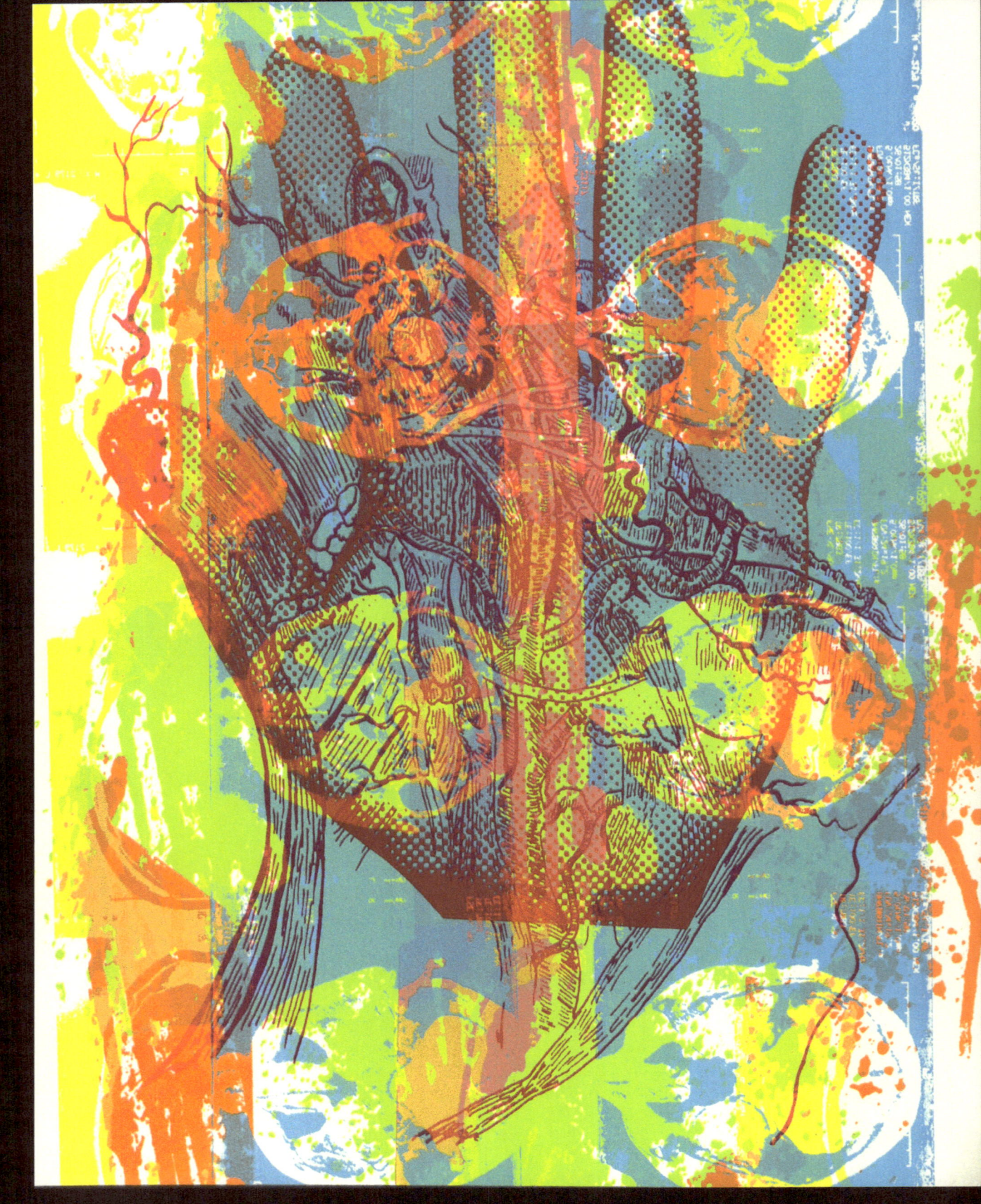

Dan Alvarado

Mind Searching, screenprint

Most of my artworks focus on the content of political satire, expressing my thoughts of the current cultural lifestyles we live through. From the political environment that have effected the United States today, to the pop culture we see, hear, eat and drink, I feel that all of this have their place in my art, which I consider humorous. Having been heavily influenced by the pop art wave in the 1960s, I also have a deep interest in the current street art/ graffiti movement that is occurring today. Through street art is an art form that has blossomed here in the United States over the past 30 years, this trend has developed itself the 'pop art' of this generation, becoming a more accepted style of art day by day. And living around, as well as following and researching this movement, I do my part of expressing myself on paintings, drawing and prints with vibrant colors used by many graffiti artists.

The print you have here for the print exchange is an example of the influence of the current graffiti movement. The usage of vibrant colors and over-layering of stencils help bring this print together. Unlike many of my political works that go straight to the point, this becomes fun and experimental on which colors I use, and the final result of each layering. The other component of this fun is the usage of x-rays as a stencil. Having the CAT scans given to me as a gift, I love the results it brings. And the beauty of the human anatomy itself I have always enjoyed viewing and working with into my art.

www.danalvarado.com

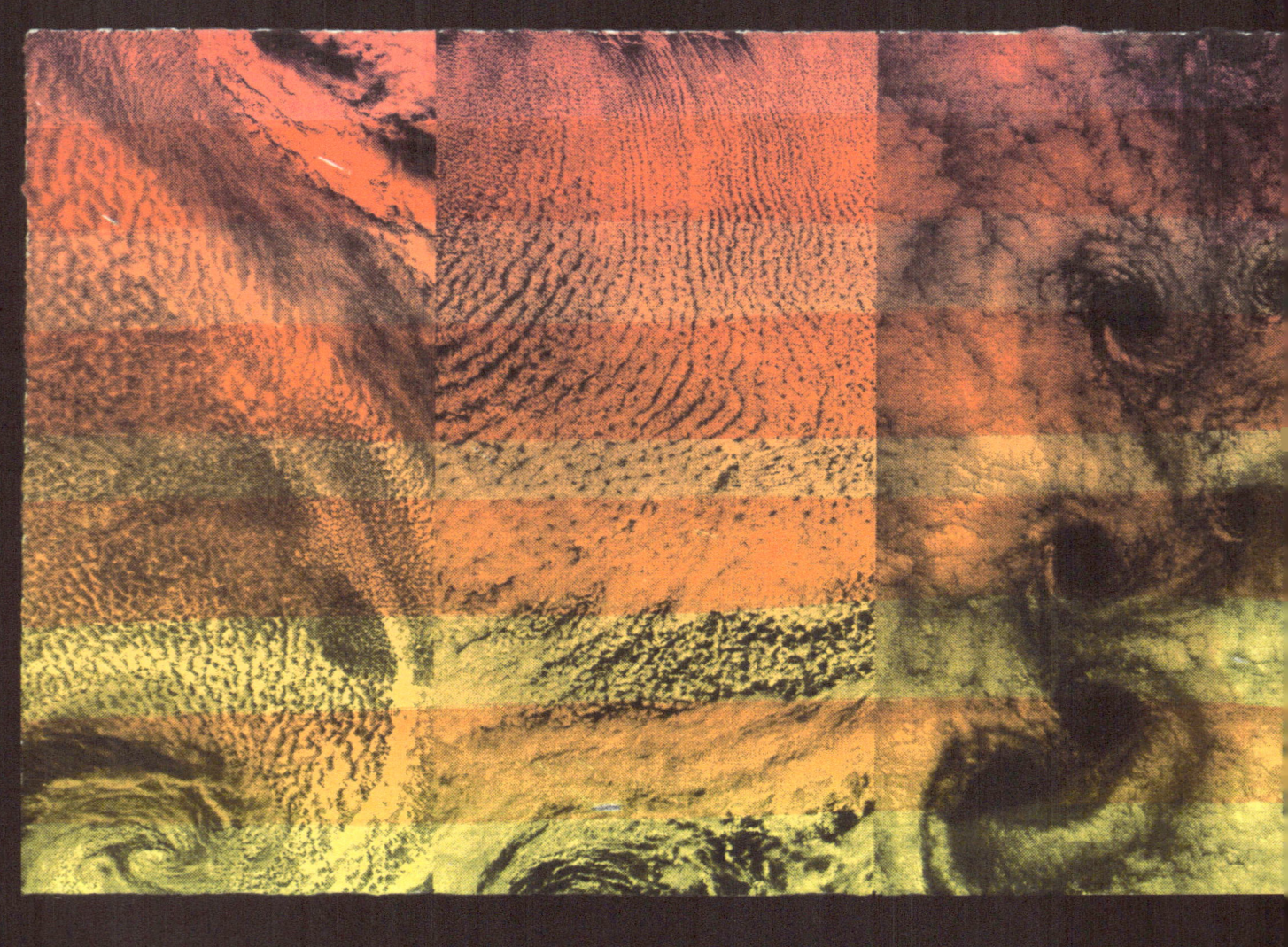

Bill Brookover

Atmospherics #3, screenprint

I discovered screen-printing in 2003 at Fleisher Art Memorial, a community-based art center in Philadelphia, PA. I was awakened to the vast creative possibilities of the medium and began studying to master the techniques. I now teach a class in screen-printing at Fleisher.

My recent work incorporates hand pulled transparent layers o ink with digital photographs I've found on the internet. I'm interested in combining the handmade with digital images available through today's sophisticated communications technology. The color layers are printed by hand, carefully pulling a blend of ink to create the color field, then repeating parts of the blend in more intense colors. The photographic imagery is from digital photographs of clouds taken by astronauts on the international space station. I download the public domain images and process them through photo software to prepare them for hand printing.

This print combines the wonder I feel in watching a sunset, which is a timeless and universal experience, with the wonder of looking down at clouds from outer space, an experience which is specific to our times.

www.Flickr.com/photos/wdb3b

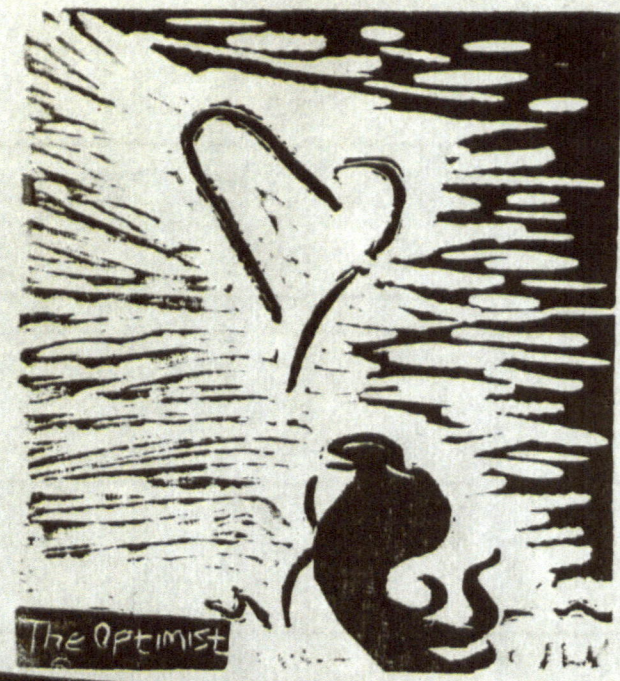

The Optimist

What goes up must come down.

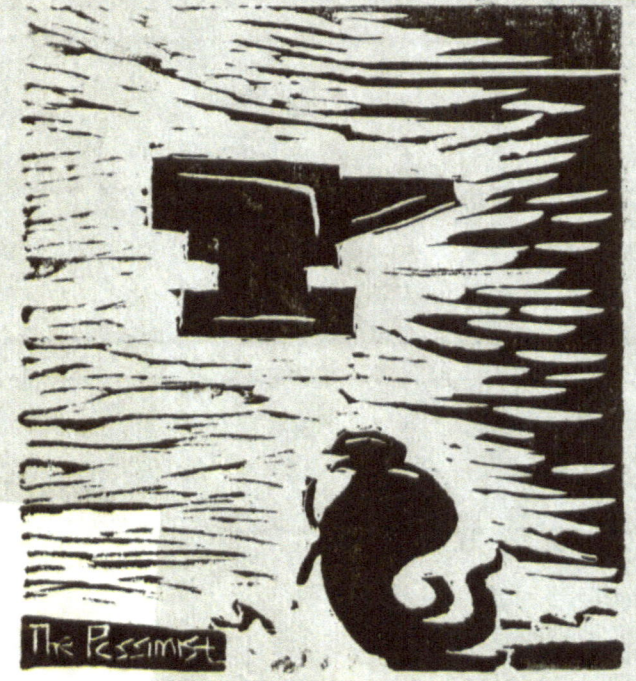

The Pessimist

Sabrina Cacciatore

What Goes Up Must Come Down, linocut

My name is Sabrina Cacciatore, and I am new to the world of printmaking. But now that I have discovered it, it is my new passion. I usually work with oil and acrylic paints as well as charcoal and graphite to portray my messages of pessimism and optimism. In the printmaking world, I have found that the linoleum is my medium of choice and greatly conveys my style in a different and more passionate way than a paintbrush or pencil and the fact that it can be replicated and shared with the world goes along beautifully with the message in my work.

I believe everyone has experienced life through pessimistic and optimistic eyes, some more intensely than others. I believe that he choice is yours and only yours to either give up on the world or keep moving forward. Whichever you choose can greatly influence all other aspects in your life. I try to not only portray the feelings within myself, but to also reflect on the audience. I want many others to be able to relate and look back on their own experiences to connect with the message and perhaps even to each other.

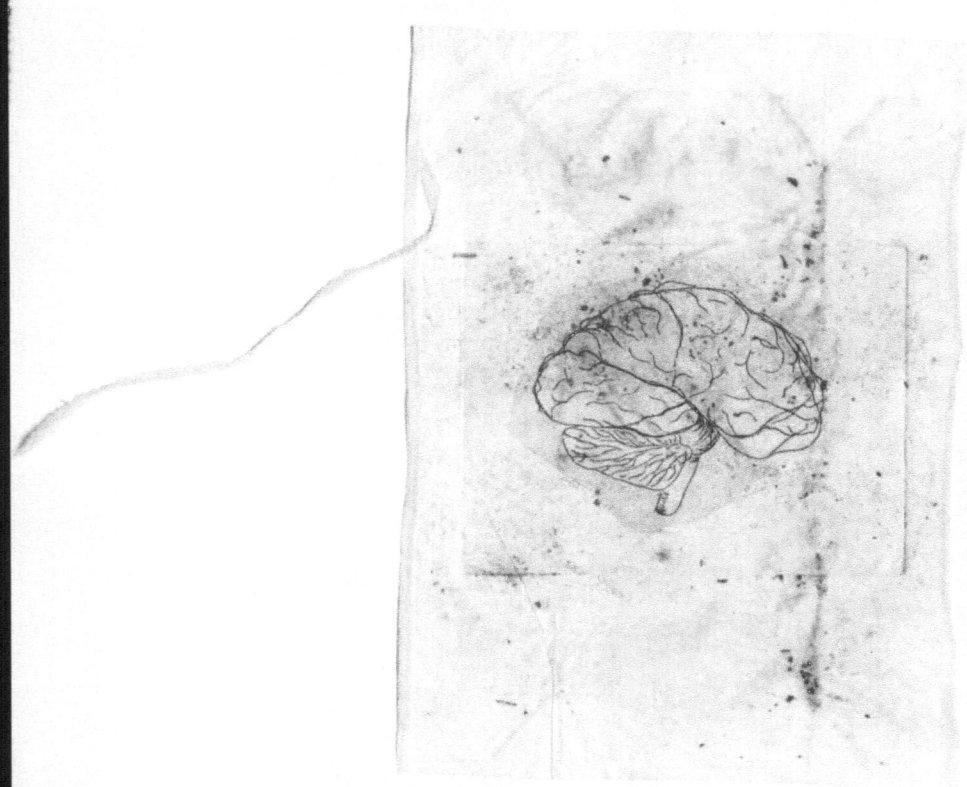

11/11   Brain Tea   Katie

Kathryn Cellerini

Brain Tea, etching, chine colle on reused tea bags

Gilles Deleuze and Felix Guattari discuss in their essay Rhizome that ideal worlds are composed of systems which are infinitely connected to adjacent or even distant systems. Brain Tea is part of an ongoing series investigating embodiment of memory in systems connected to the neurological.

The human body subconsciously (and sometimes consciously) responds positively and negatively to our daily interactions. Sometimes memories of these interactions are so powerful that the body will react physically to them as well. Body and memory are thus inseparable and the vast array of chronic disorders such as anxiety, depression, and in my case, Ulcerative Colitis, are linked to one's ability to cope with stress.

www.kathryncellerini.com

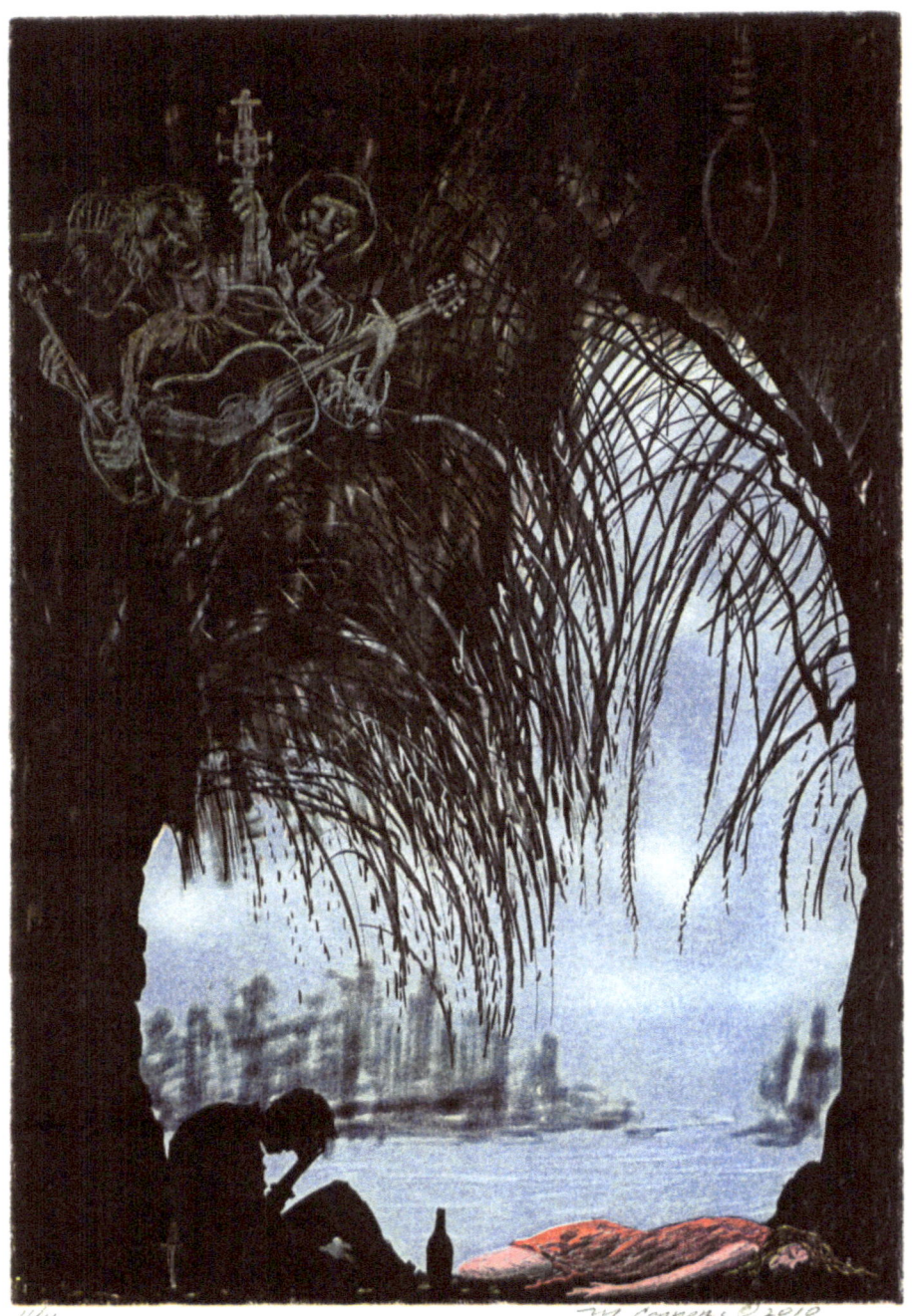

11/11   W. Connors © 2010

Michael Connors

Down In The Willow Garden, lithograph

I play guitar in jam bands in the Madison, Wisconsin area. I am interested in the folk stories that are told through song- especially those old songs that re-tell the human dramas of personal relationships.

Not all relationships go wrong, but in the case of *Down in the Willow Garden*, things go terribly wrong: a man murders a woman because she will not marry him. This print visualizes one specific line of the song: *"I gave her a bottle of burgundy wine; my love she did not know… and that's where I poisoned that dear little girl, down on the banks below."* Later in the song it is revealed that his primary motive to marry her was for money.

Because I do a lot of singing, I use pictures like these in my mind to remember all of the lyrics.

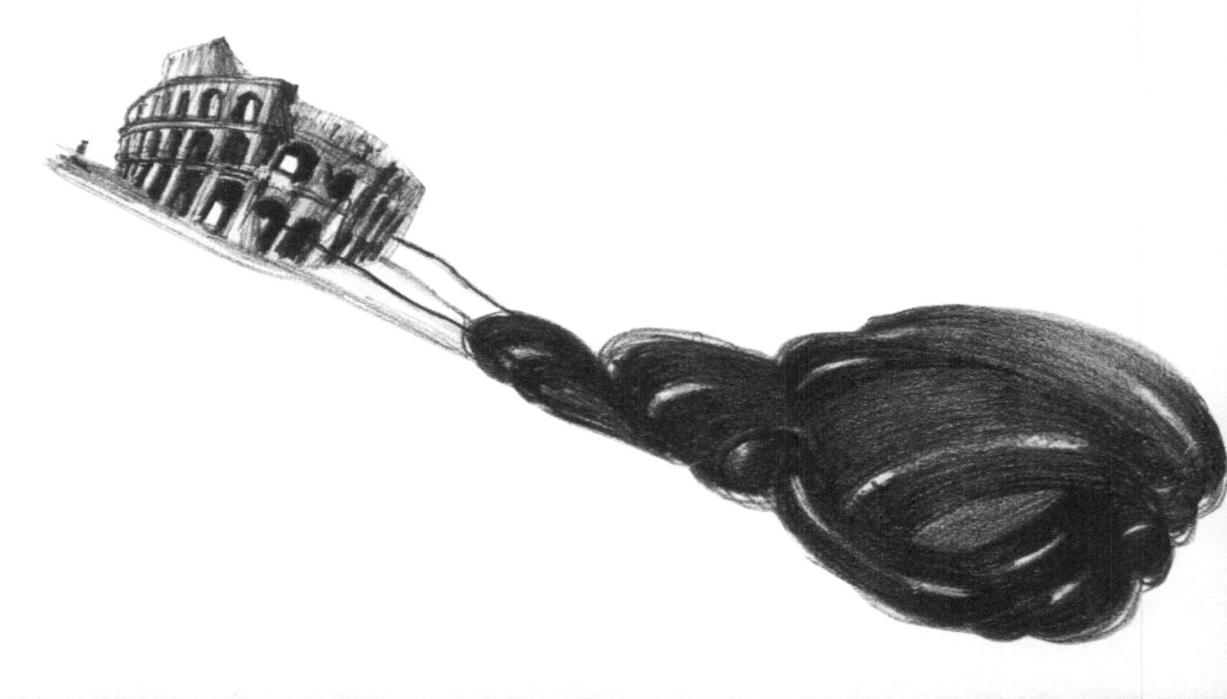

Aimee Denault

Questionable History, lithograph

I currently make prints and drawings. My main concern is technique and concept. I use traditional methods of drawing to express a range of ideas. During my undergraduate studies emphasis was placed on drawing proficiency, anatomy and the understanding what we see on an intellectual and visual level. My current work applies this training to explore ways of combining material and forms common in our everyday lives in unconventional ways to create depth and expand visual content. I manipulate and ply with common subjects, without regard for physics and material properties, in order to challenge routine perceptions. My drawings or prints look "normal" from a certain distance but morph into something unexpected otherwise. Introducing fanciful distortion and impossible configurations of common items are key elements of my artwork.

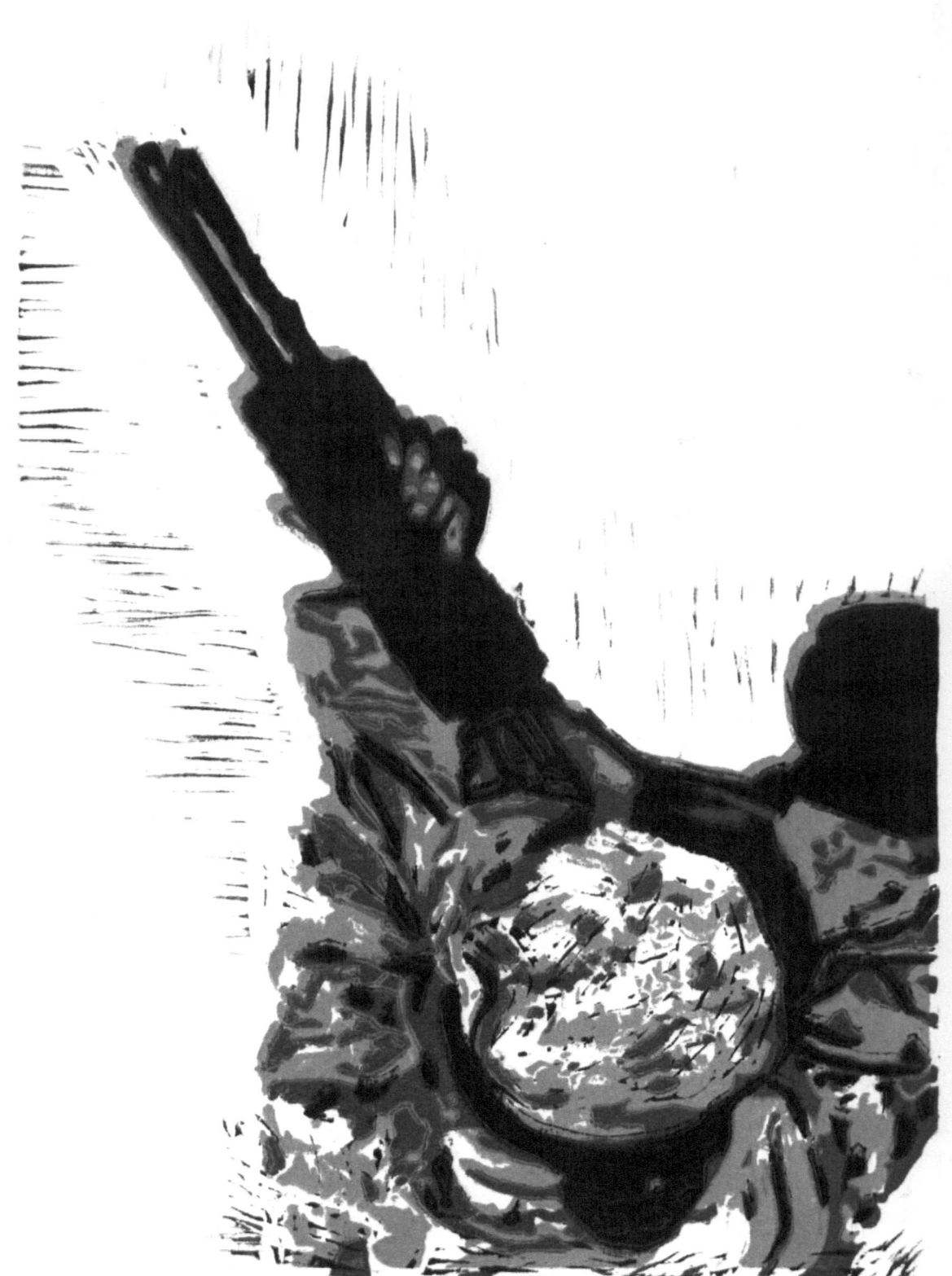

11/11   UNDER FIRE   ESTHER '10

Esther Kwon

Under Fire, reduction linocut

World War I, World War II, Vietnam, Korea, 9/11, Iraq: Wars affect people, families, and their lifestyles. Does it affect art? I consider art a communication tool for artists to express themselves. As a minority female Marine, I always feel the need to prove myself.

My experiences of war, and the personal relationships I found along the way, are portrayed in my work. Defined as a woman through tightly tied hair buns, I strive to distinguish myself in this man's world. What may look like mundane activities to us may create another meaning when taken out of its milieu.

Under Fire is a feminist view of the military. Highlighting the rifle, the hair bun, and her shadow, it is a woman. As women are not allowed in the infantry, *Under Fire* is a propaganda showing a female Marine in a foxhole, stating that women can fight in the fronts just like men. The offset registration creates a vibration underground, just as it would if mortars hit nearby the foxhole. It is this motion that inspires the title.

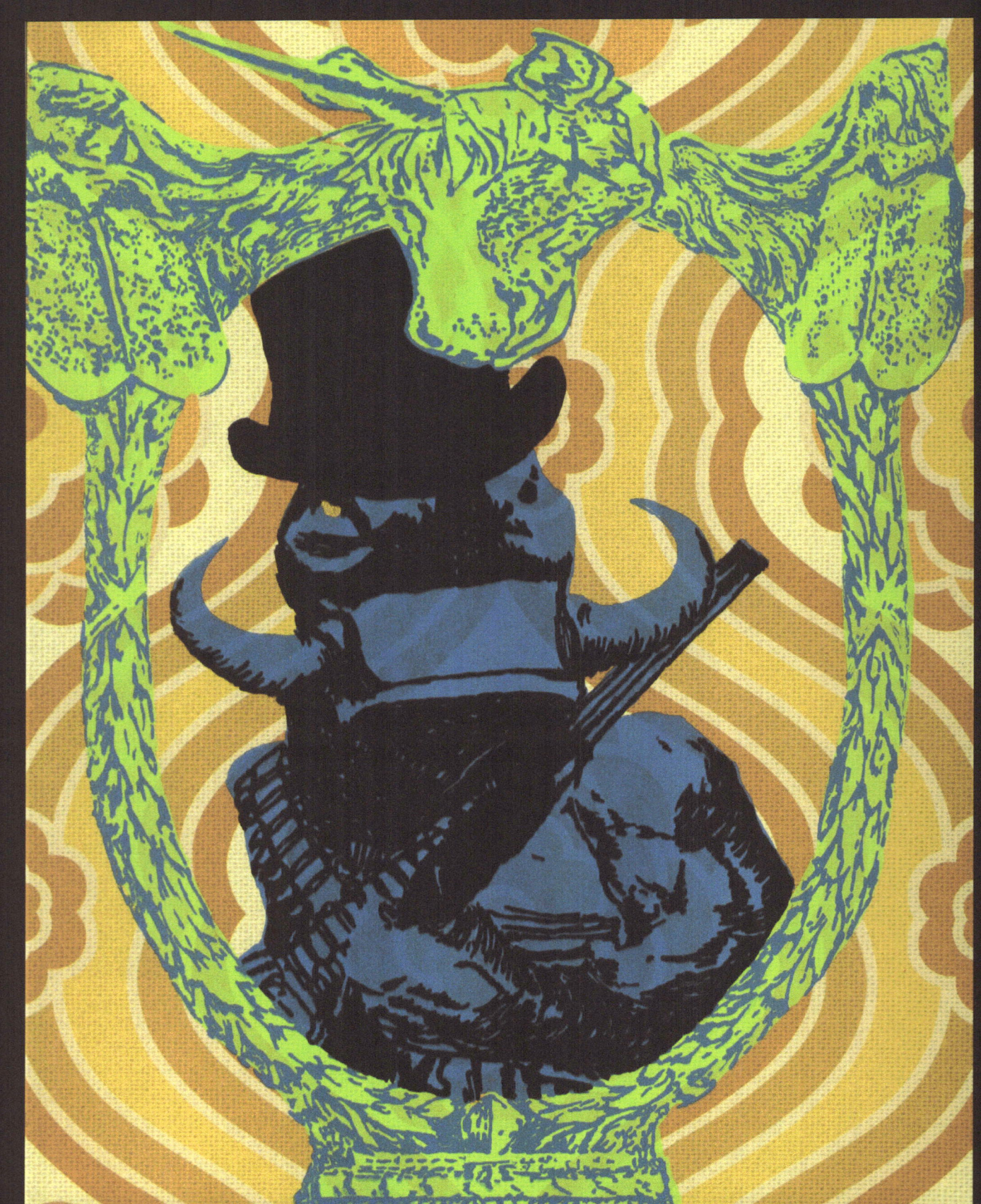

Justin Mages

Brigadier General Melvin, wallpaper, gold leaf, screenprint

My background in fine arts is primarily painting based. Only recently have I really been exploring screenprinting to create my art. One of the things that I enjoy most about printmaking is the ability for my work to spread to a larger group of people in an easier, more economical way than painting could offer me or my viewers.

All of the layers in my prints are hand drawn. I do this so my work does not become disconnected from me. This is one of the ways that I manage to integrate my painting background into my printmaking. The organic process of screen printing can sometimes become cumbersome, so I sometimes use Photoshop or Illustrator. Using digital technologies allows me to be able to have a better guess at how the different layers will interact with each other. I always enjoy working to get the layers to play well together, more than designing hte initial concept itself.

One of the major recurring themes in my work is updating elements from historical printmaking, which essentially allows me to create my own history with fictional characters. I give the viewer a chance to consider how history has been taught to them, while simultaneously allowing them to create a new history that could be more real or meaningful to them.

www.etsy.com/shop/justinmages

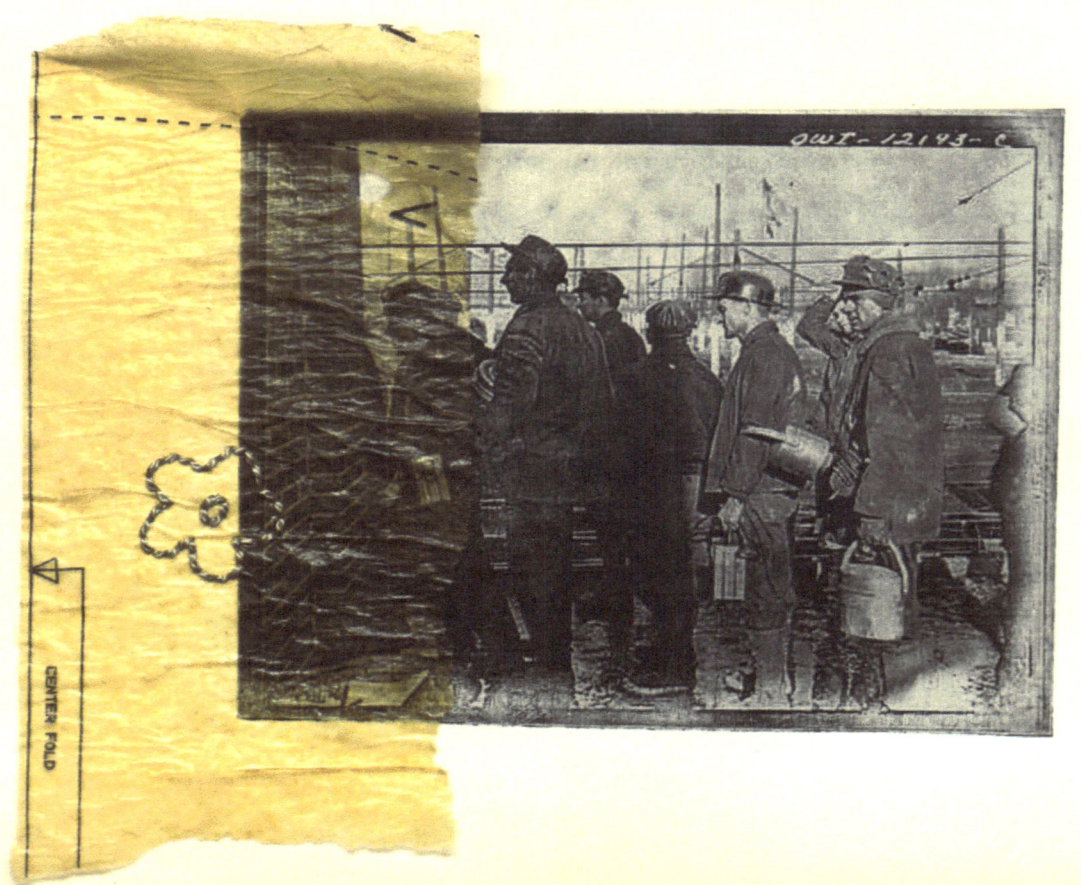

Alisha McCurdy

Mother, Father, Daughter; monotype solarplate on BFK w/ sewing pattern & embroidery

Family is a fragile, complicated entity, requiring a delicate balance of its members to sustain itself. A thin thread wraps around each individual, looping to connect parents to child, child to sibling; often, the thread can stretch too tightly, or have too much slack. The instances during which family balance is knocked off center and the subsequent attempts to restore the stability are of interest in my work. Using materials that have strong connections with domestic craft alongside harder materials of wood and metal, give rise to concerns of locating place between masculine and feminine traditions of work and underscore familial tensions. www.alishamccurdy.com

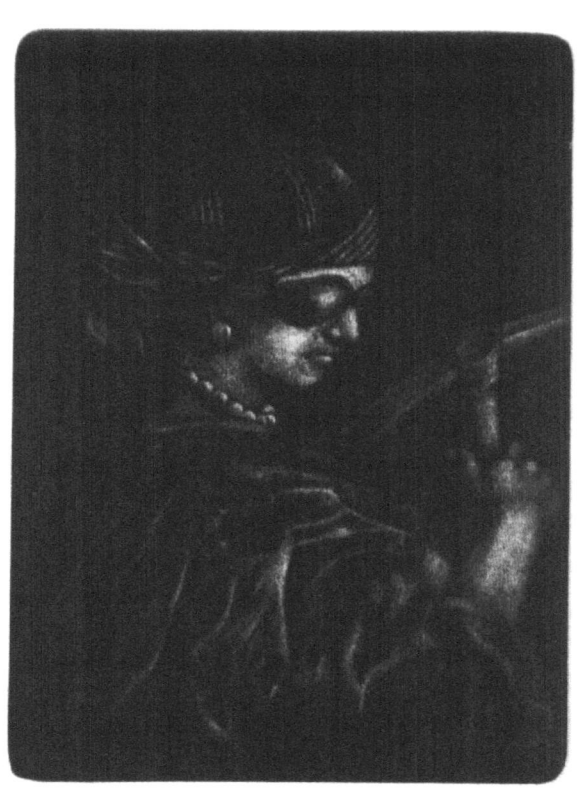

Aaron Miller

Breaker, mezzotint

In this image, entitled *Breaker,* I am highlighting the disparity between the miner and the historical upper class. Here, I juxtapose a "mask" of a contemporary miner over a neo-classical portrait. This mezzotint plays with our cultural legacy, quoting the inventors of the Renaissance as well as the gentleman class of the Industrial Revolution. The tools and machines and event the spirit of inquiry of these periods would eventually lead to the current alarming conditions of our environment. At first glance these images read as portraits from some historic estate. However, after a moment's observation, the viewer notices the head lamp or pickaxe of a miner.
www.aaronmillerart.com

face to face

fredoth 10

Jose Antonio Ojeda

Face to Face, metal cutout embossment on BFK

Jose Antonio Ojeda is a current MFA student at Stony Brook University, having received his BA form Dartmouth College. He works with a wide range of mediums, including painting, print-making, installation, and metal work. As a Bronx, NY native of Ecuadorian descent, a lot of his art deals with the excavation of identity- striving to resurrect an ancient history and heritage within a modern context. He is interested in the power of community and in how much we can learn from each other and our respective cultures and experiences. Pop culture icons from his youth make their way into his work, combined with the symbols and icons of various world cultures. There is a particular interest in dualities of being, becoming a hybrid (as with an animal or a machine) for the hopes of improvement. While a lot of his work is self referential, he hopes that a viewer can find the link and relate it to their own experiences.
www.joseojeda.com

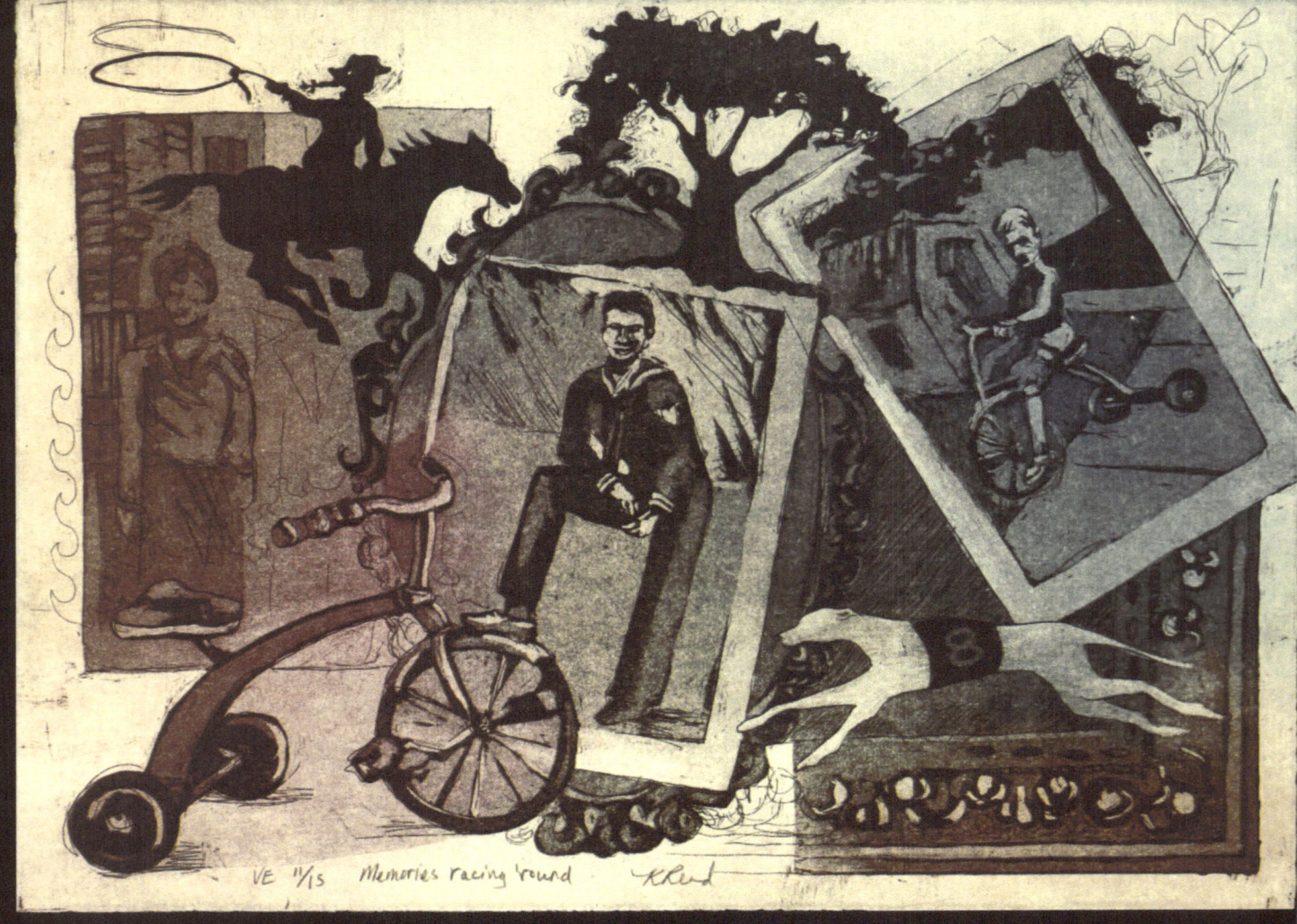

VE 11/15   Memories racing 'round   KReid

Krystal Read

Memories Racing 'Round, intaglio

My artwork explores the fantasies and ambiguities revealed by the act of remembering. After stumbling upon a collection of old photographs at an antique store, I was drawn by the mystery of the photos. The discarded treasures that clutter our attics and fill antique stores inspire me to investigate and imbue these objects with my own fantasies.

The intaglio print, *Memories Racing 'Round*, represents the past as it becomes morphed by our own imagination. The memories break outside their confined borders and become interrelated, entangled, and nonsensical. Some memories appear clear, some remain fuzzy, and some are just thin lines of incomplete information.

www.krystalread.com

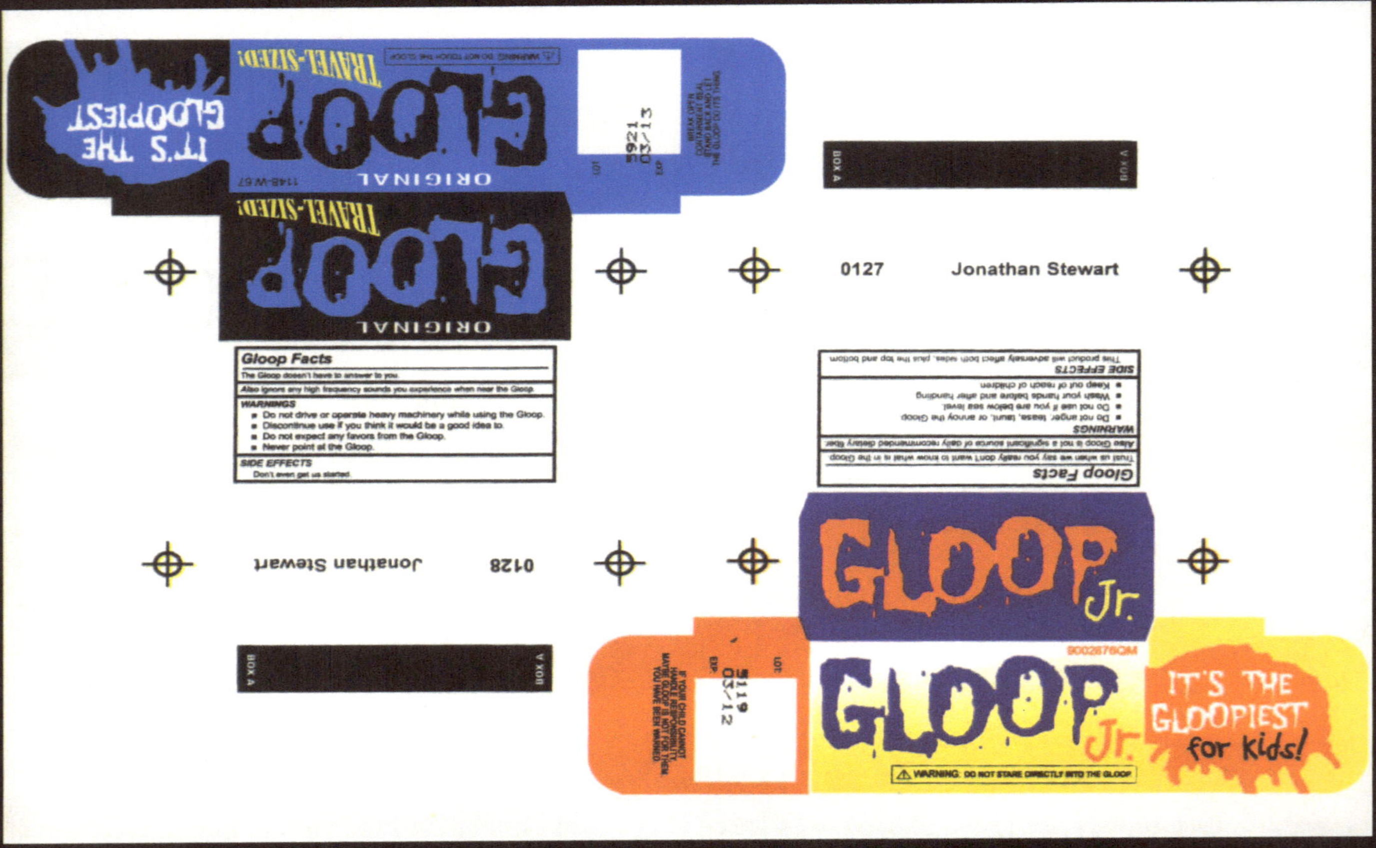

GLOOP
ORIGINAL
TRAVEL-SIZED!
IT'S THE GLOOPIEST

GLOOP
ORIGINAL
TRAVEL-SIZED!

LOT 5921
EXP 03/13

Gloop Facts

The Gloop doesn't have to answer to you.

Also ignore any high frequency sounds you experience when near the Gloop.

WARNINGS
- Do not drive or operate heavy machinery while using the Gloop.
- Discontinue use if you think it would be a good idea to.
- Do not expect any favors from the Gloop.
- Never point at the Gloop.

SIDE EFFECTS
Don't even get us started.

BOX A

0127   Jonathan Stewart

0128   Jonathan Stewart

BOX A

Gloop Facts

Trust us when we say you really don't want to know what is in the Gloop.

Also Gloop is not a significant source of daily recommended dietary fiber.

WARNINGS
- Do not anger, tease, taunt, or annoy the Gloop
- Do not use if you are below sea level
- Wash your hands before and after handling
- Keep out of reach of children

SIDE EFFECTS
This product will adversely affect both sides, plus the top and bottom

GLOOP Jr.

GLOOP Jr.

9002878QM

IT'S THE GLOOPIEST for kids!

LOT 5119
EXP 03/12

⚠ WARNING: DO NOT STARE DIRECTLY INTO THE GLOOP

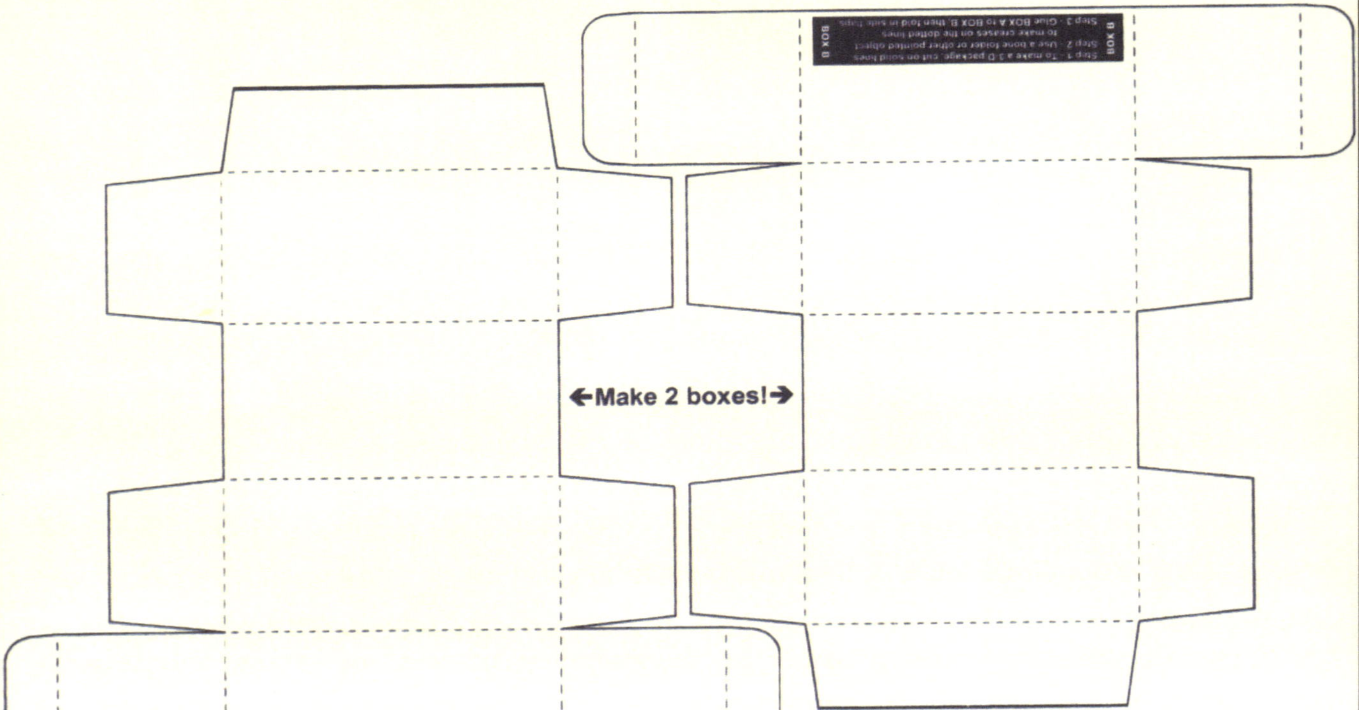

Make 2 boxes!

BOX B

Step 1 - To make a 3-D package, cut on solid lines
Step 2 - Use a bone folder or other pointed object to make creases on the dotted lines
Step 3 - Glue BOX A to BOX B, then fold in side flaps

BOX B

Name: Jonathan Stewart
Title: Gloop Jr / Gloop Travel-Sized
Medium: Ink on paper
Process: Screenprint
Wheat Farm Press Print Exchange 1:1

Jonathan Stewart

Gloop Jr. & Gloop Travel-Sized, screenprint

I am worried about what is contained in some of the things you can buy to put in or on your body, whether it is food, medicine, or cosmetics. Gloop is the illogical extension.
Follow the directions on the back of the print to make these folded boxes.

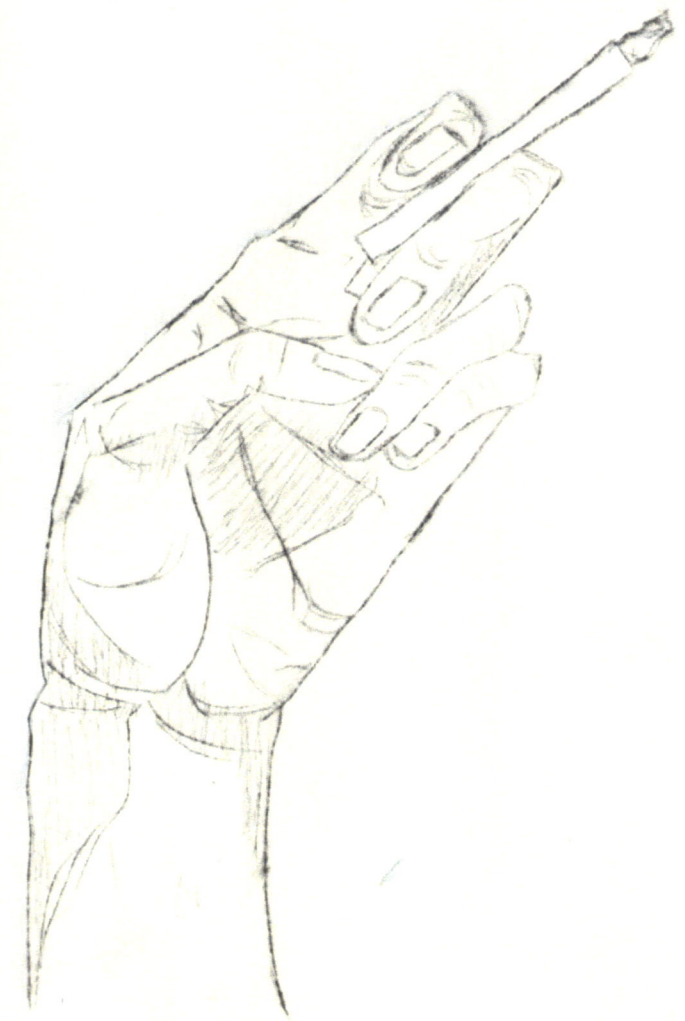

11/11   It was Always Our thing

Nicole Suchy

It Was Always Our Thing, ink, gesso and watercolor

Art making will always be a very stress relieving focused process. As a vehicle, it enables the expressions of moments, thoughts, and otherwise inexpressible experiences such as communication barriers, and interpersonal relationships. I am very interested in the secrets and struggles that lie behind objects, moments, and words. After my brother's incarceration, communication themes popped up all throughout my work.

For two and a half years, he and I have been left with nothing but letter writing as a means of communication; this forced, altered relationship between us drives my obsessive attempts to recreate and solidify all of the moments we have lost.

I am interested in themes of memory, absence, loss, and miscommunication. My work explores isolated moment and the failed attempts to reconstruct, alter, or preserve theses memories.

www.nicolerosesuchy.com

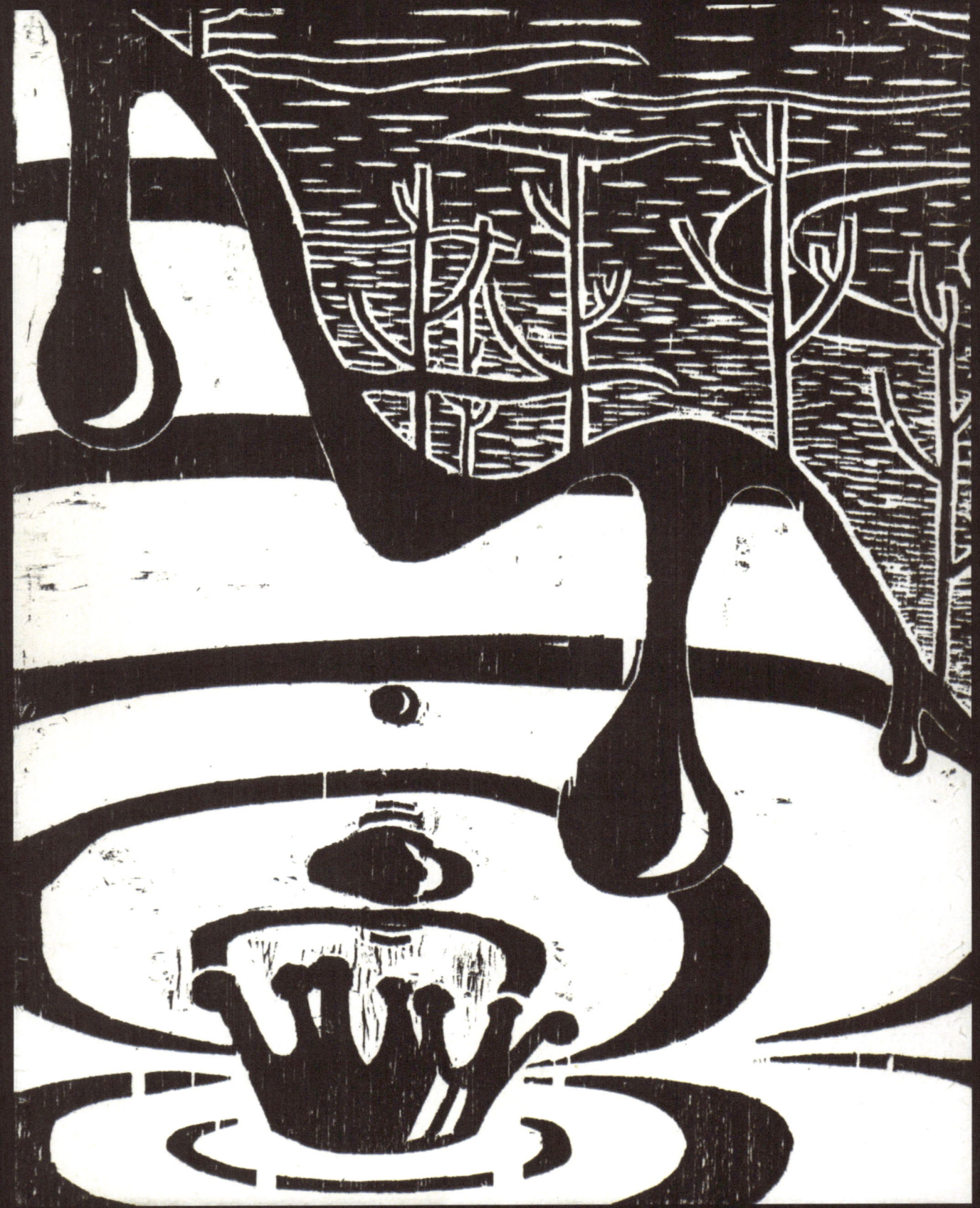

Ariana Warner

Grain, woodblock

Almost all of my work portrays imagery that is personal, whether that is reflected by portraits of people in my life, events that have changed my life or has a connection with who I am as a person.

In "*Grain*", the main basis is that everything in nature is repetitive and that you can find similarities even amongst things that are very different. The core texture of wood, its grain, can be found repeatedly throughout the natural world creating nature's pattern. It can be found in the ripples of the water, in the dirt of a mountain, and even within a cloudy sky. Grain also when looked at in a particular manner becomes the rings of a tree. Rings of a tree tell you its age, which represents the constancy of time. Everything has its own time frame and even though each object's time may overlap, each object experiences something different because of the constant change within the present.

Right now in my life, since I'm in college, it is a joining of the all these different people at various times in our lives that "overlapping" and interacting with each other. We, as individuals are constantly changing, evolving, growing. Each of us affects one another as a ripple in a pool of water. We all come together, each of us a single grain of dirt that combines to form a mountain. Though all of us are different, we are ever changing as a cloud.

In college, I have enjoyed meeting so many new and unique people that have greatly affected my life. Now as an upper classman, many of my friends are graduating and I realize life will never be the same, which regardless of us being around each other, our lives separately will continue. These changes will alter the relationships. Now that we are no longer "moving together" it is more difficult to relate to each other, just as the sky cannot relate to the mountain or the life of a still pool of water. People need to look at how we're similar and not focus on just the differences because at the end of the day we should all be able to relate in some way, shape or form just as the sky, mountain, and water all can through it's grain.

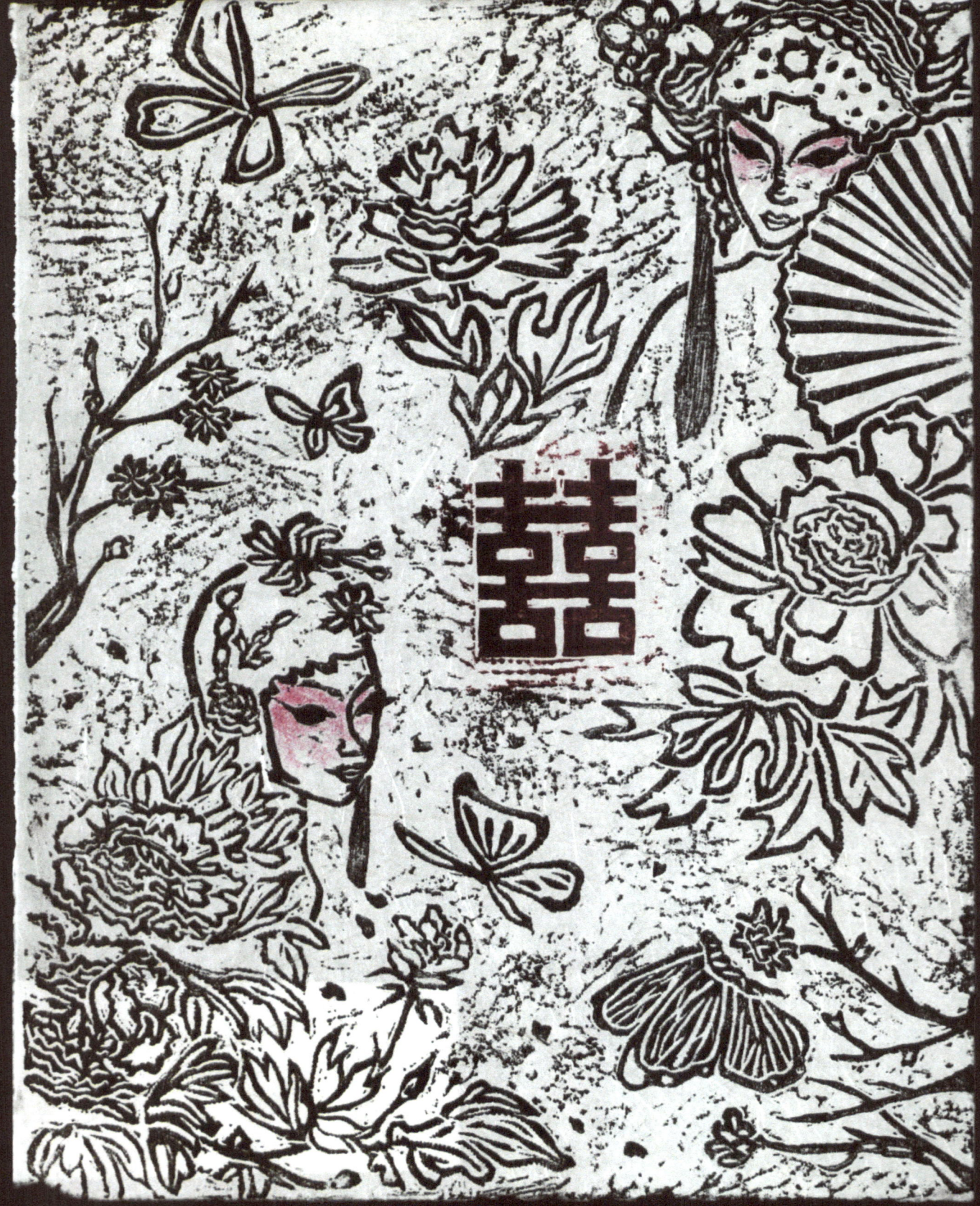

Si Wu

Peerless, linocut

Most of my art work is about the cultural and natural issues, but I also take a critical view of social and political issues. In my work, I deconstruct the Chinese fairy tales, plants, Chinese dream, and nursery rhymes, these are all part of my childhood and ancient Chinese culture, and I also combine Chinese culture and American culture together. I work in series, all my art works can not only be considered as a single piece, but also have connection with each other, and they all have strong personal meaning. Each of my projects often consists of multiple works, usually in a range of different media, grouped around specific themes and meanings.